World Series Champions: Oakland Athletics

Pitcher Jim "Catfish" Hunter

Pitcher Tim Hudson

WORLD SERIES CHAMPIONS

OAKLAND
ATHLETICS

JOE TISCHLER

CREATIVE EDUCATION / CREATIVE PAPERBACKS

CREATIVE
SPORTS

Published by Creative Education and Creative Paperbacks
P.O. Box 227, Mankato, Minnesota 56002
Creative Education and Creative Paperbacks are imprints of
The Creative Company
www.thecreativecompany.us

Art Direction by Tom Morgan
Book production by Ciara Beitlich
Edited by Jill Kalz

Photographs by AP Images (John Hefti), Corbis (B Bennett, Don
Smith), Getty (The Conlon Collection, Focus on Sport, Otto Greule
Jr., Thearon W. Henderson, Al Messerschmidt, MLB Photos, National
Baseball Hall of Fame, George Rinhart, Jim Rogash, Jamie Squire)

Library of Congress Cataloging-in-Publication Data
Names: Tischler, Joe, author.
Title: Oakland Athletics / Joe Tischler.
Description: Mankato, MN : Creative Education and Creative
    Paperbacks, 2024. | Series: Creative sports. World Series
    champions | Includes index. | Audience: Ages 7-10 | Audience:
    Grades 2-3 | Summary: "Elementary-level text and engaging
    sports photos highlight the Oakland Athletics' MLB World Series
    wins and losses, plus sensational players associated with the
    professional baseball team such as Barry Zito."-- Provided by
    publisher.
Identifiers: LCCN 2023011768 (print) | LCCN 2023011769 (ebook)
    | ISBN 9781640268319 (library binding) | ISBN 9781682773819
    (paperback) | ISBN 9781640269842 (pdf)
Subjects: LCSH: Oakland Athletics (Baseball team)--History--
    Juvenile literature. | World Series (Baseball)--History--Juvenile
    literature.
Classification: LCC GV875.024 T57 2024 (print) | LCC GV875.024
    (ebook) | DDC 796.357/640979466--dc23/eng/20230330
LC record available at https://lccn.loc.gov/2023011768
LC ebook record available at https://lccn.loc.gov/2023011769

Printed in China

tcher Rollie Fingers

CONTENTS

Home of the Athletics

Oakland, California, is a vibrant city near the Pacific Ocean. The Athletics baseball team plays its home games there. The team is often called the "A's." Players and fans love soaking up the sun in a **stadium** called Oakland-Alameda County Coliseum.

The Oakland Athletics are a Major League Baseball (MLB) team. They compete in the American League (AL) West Division. Their **rivals** are the Los Angeles Angels. All MLB teams want to win the World Series and become champions. The A's have done so nine times!

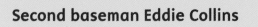
Second baseman Eddie Collins

Naming the Athletics

akland is the Athletics' third home. The club started in Philadelphia, Pennsylvania, and later went to Kansas City, Missouri. They have been called Athletics in all three cities. The name comes from the Athletic Club of Philadelphia, the city's first amateur baseball team.

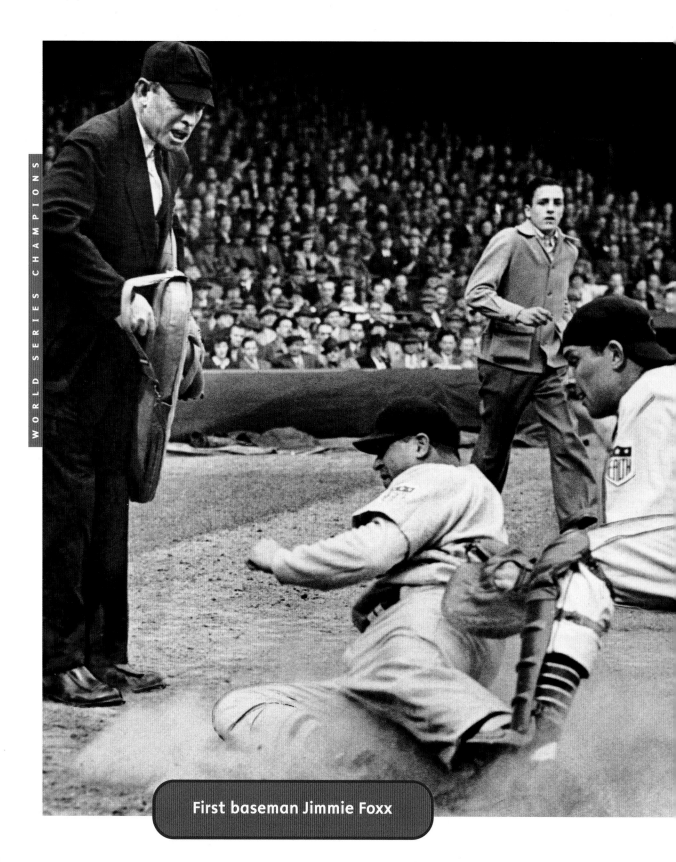

First baseman Jimmie Foxx

Athletics History

The AL was formed in 1901. The Athletics were one of its first teams. They were winners right away. They won the AL **pennant** in 1902. Eddie Collins and John "Home Run" Baker were two early hitting stars. They helped the team win three World Series **titles** from 1910 to 1913.

The A's won three straight AL pennants from 1929 to 1931. They won two more World Series, too. Jimmie Foxx belted a lot of home runs. Left-hander Robert "Lefty" Grove struck out batters.

Then the A's fell into a big **slump**. They moved to Kansas City in 1955 and Oakland in 1968. They finally made the **playoffs** again in 1971. They appeared in the World Series three straight years from 1972 to 1974—and won all three! Outfielder Reggie Jackson drove in many runs. He played in six All-Star games as an Athletic. He also won an AL Most Valuable Player (MVP) Award.

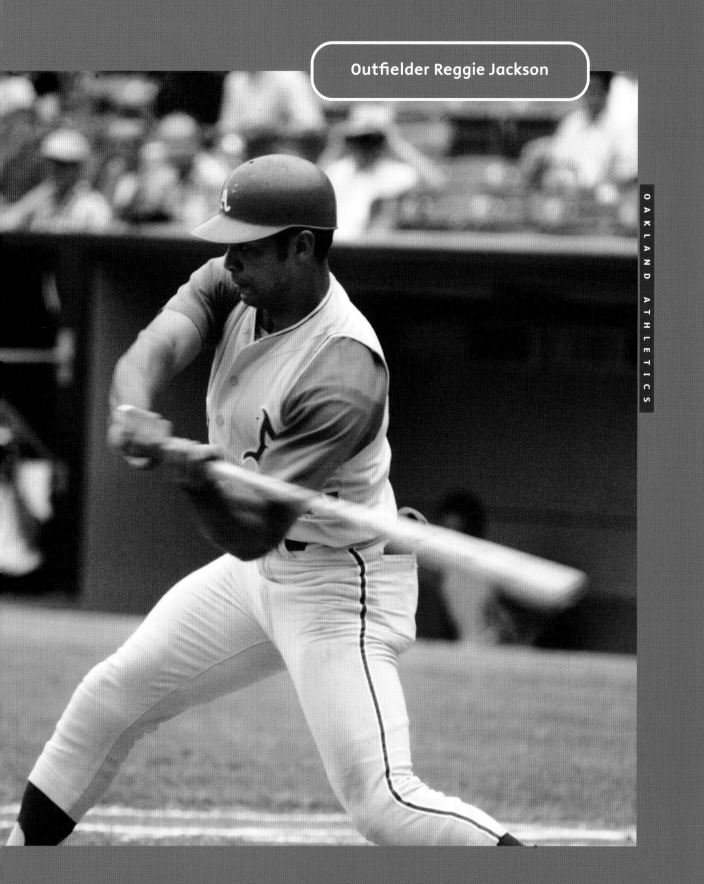

Outfielder Reggie Jackson

Outfielder José Canseco

First baseman Mark McGwire

O akland reached three more World Series from 1988 to 1990. They won their ninth title in 1989. They swept the San Francisco Giants. Sluggers Mark McGwire and José Canseco were known as the "Bash Brothers." They hit baseballs hard and hit them far.

Other Athletics Stars

The A's have had plenty of stars. Outfielder Rickey Henderson stole a lot of bases. No one else in baseball stole more than him. The field at Oakland-Alameda County Coliseum is named in his honor.

Pitcher Eddie Plank won more than 300 games. He's in the Baseball **Hall of Fame**. In the 2000s, pitchers Tim Hudson and Barry Zito were standouts.

Outfielder Rickey Henderson

Pitcher Paul Blackburn

ll-Star pitcher Paul Blackburn is a new leader. So is infielder Seth Brown. Fans hope they can help bring a championship to Oakland-Alameda County Coliseum soon.

About the Athletics

Started playing: 1901

....

League/division: American League, West Division

....

Team colors: green and gold

....

Home stadium: Oakland-Alameda
  County Coliseum

....

WORLD SERIES CHAMPIONSHIPS:

  1910, 4 games to 1 over Chicago Cubs

....

  1911, 4 games to 2 over New York Giants

....

  1913, 4 games to 1 over New York Giants

....

  1929, 4 games to 1 over Chicago Cubs

....

  1930, 4 games to 2 over St. Louis Cardinals

....

  1972, 4 games to 3 over Cincinnati Reds

....

  1973, 4 games to 3 over New York Mets

....

  1974, 4 games to 1 over Los Angeles Dodgers

....

  1989, 4 games to 0 over San Francisco Giants

....

Oakland Athletics website:
  www.mlb.com/athletics

....

Glossary

Hall of Fame—a museum in which the best players of all time are honored

....

pennant—a league championship; a team that wins a pennant gets to play in the World Series

....

playoffs—games that the best teams play after a regular season to see who the champion will be

....

rival—a team that plays extra hard against another team

....

slump—a period of time when a team loses more games than it wins

....

stadium—a building with tiers of seats for spectators

....

title—another word for championship

....

Pitcher Barry Zito

Index